To Sunny and George
Christmas 1982 from
The Hjelts

JAMAICAN HOUSES
a vanishing legacy

drawings by
Anghelen Arrington Phillips

text by
Geoffrey de Sola Pinto

First Edition 2,400 copies
100 limited edition

Layout, typeset and printed by Stephensons Litho Press Ltd., Kingston, Jamaica.

Binding by Stationery Manufacturers Ltd.

DEDICATION

This book is dedicated to two very important people.

To Annabella Ogden, without who's push and caring a lot of good projects would never happen. Especially this one.

And to my daughter, Kybran A. Phillips who allowed her mother to leave her all these months, without guilt.

FOREWORD

Very sensibly, the compilers of this book have not confined their attention to the plantation-style great house — which is, in the popular belief, the only architecture of real distinction and originality in the island. At least, portrayals and descriptions of the Jamaican house tend to emphasise almost exclusively the great house — generally on a hill — surrounded by sugar cane or rolling pasture land.

Up to a point this is a fair view. The Jamaican economy in its most prosperous era did rest on the cane field and the cattle pen; and dominating each estate was the commodious, solid and often elegant proprietor's house — not only a home for the family, but the busy administrative centre for the district, the principal focus of social life, very much an excellent hotel where friends of the owner and travellers of quality would lodge free for days and even weeks at a time. In 1820 there were well over a thousand properties in Jamaica large enough to carry over one hundred slaves or head of stock or both. Nearly thirty of these estates were holdings over five hundred slaves or six hundred and fifty head of stock. Demesnes, that is, on a truly baronial scale, with great houses to match their economic and social significance.

But these splendidly impressive products of the 'middle' period of Jamaican architecture — about 1760 to 1820 — are not the only valuable part of Jamaica's architectural heritage. Indeed, they are only a part of what the late Tom Concannon called the 'vernacular' of a distinctive Jamaican architectural style. Around them — and continuing after them when Emancipation and the decline of sugar brought their building to a halt — was a vigorous tradition of comely, practical and, above all, comfortable domestic architecture which should be recorded and understood. The great house may have inspired this tradition; but the great house itself is an extension, an enlarged example, of this tradition.

As I suggested above, this tradition seems to have established itself about the middle of the Eighteenth Century. Before this — except for a few example such as Vale Royal (St. Andrew), Stokes Hall (St. Thomas), Colbeck Castle (St. Catherine), the Seville Great House (St. Ann), the sugar factory at Kenilworth (Hanover) and the joined house-factory complex at Ladyfield (St. Thomas) — building was largely make-shift, and there are not enough enduring examples of the early period, from 1655 to 1760, sufficiently preserved to be useful except to scholars or to justify expert and faithful restoration.

The later period — from just before Emancipation — seems to have come to an end in the early 1930s.There has been a great deal of private (and a measure of government) restoration and reconditioning of buildings in the tradition. But there have been very few new attempts in it. Almost any substantial house over fifty years old in the corporate area is one of a protected species; and any new owner of it, or of lands and buildings adjacent, has to get government approval before it is altered or before buildings out of character are erected around it.

Certainly, very few of the huge upper and middle-class and tourist developments built since 1945 contain more than a slight element of the three century tradition we can trace between 1655 and the first three decades of the Twentieth Century.

"Jamaican Houses, a vanishing legacy", is a valuable and innovative work, not only for the sensitivity and accuracy of the drawings and the well-summarised information contained in the accompanying text but for the scope of the examples chosen to represent our architectural tradition.

It covers nearly three hundred years — from Vale Royal (about 1694) to the Norton House (about 1930). Rose Hall (about 1750), the overseer's house at Cardiff Hall (mid-eighteenth century), George Stiebel's Devon House (1881), the house on Market Street, Montego Bay (1910) and Neuville (1922) are confident assertions of a reassuring continuity. People have evidently been building with conscience — and with intention to stay — for a long time in Jamaica. These houses all declare a happy claiming and possession of the place.

And this act of possession is, perhaps, the most attractive feature of this book. Each one of the structures featured within has been in continuous use since the day of its building — whether as a habitation or as a place for educating people (Mico), for selling people things they need (the store in Lucea), for public service (the Railway Station, Port Antonio). Some of them, like Rose Hall, have changed function; but they are all active centres for living or trading or administering or increasing skills.

They are silent witnesses to the fact that there is an enduring tradition of Jamaican architecture; a tradition that tried to marry a handsome aesthetic and utilitarian purpose.

It is a tradition we might consider studying for a little and applying to our own domestic and public creations, a lot of people in our past built not only for shelter but with a careful regard for what would complement and enhance the varied beauty of their landscape.

John Hearne
Chairman
Institute of Jamaica

LOCATIONS OF BUILDINGS

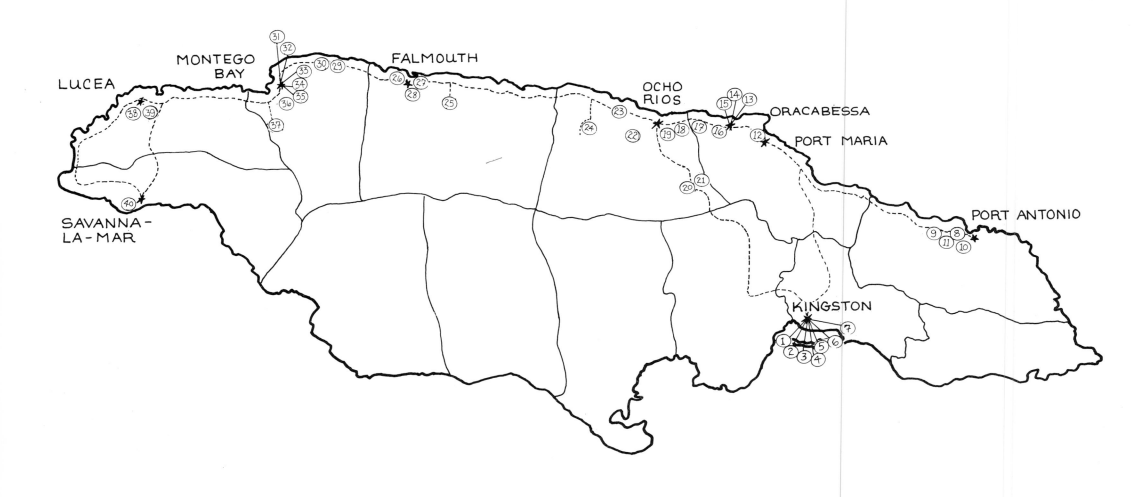

INDEX

1   DEVON HOUSE, Hope Road, Kingston

This classic mansion was built in 1881 by George Stiebel who became Custos of St. Andrew. Born in Kingston in 1820, he was apprenticed to a wheelwright but later travelled extensively in South America making his fortune in gold mining.

His family lived in this house for over forty years as did a later owner, Cecil Lindo, whose wealth came from sugar and rum. His widow lived here until her death in 1967 and her austere family butler, Jackson, a tall and elegant old man, in livery, met all who came to the door. In that year, the Jamaica National Trust acquired the building for the government and restored it as a centre for the craft industry. For some years it housed the National Gallery but it has now reverted to showrooms for Things Jamaican. Many colourful Craft Fairs were organised in the courtyard behind the house by Sally Asher.

The present house was constructed on the site of a former one known as Devon Pen and the coach house and silver vault, to the left of this building, date from then, as do some of the many out-houses flanking the large grass courtyard at the rear.

Behind this beautifully balanced wooden facade in the Georgian manner, is a brick fabric. Erected on monumental scale, this house, with its high ceilings, elegant mahogany staircases, panelling and doorways, has a fine drawing room upstairs with a covered ceiling embelished with plasterwork. In a temperate climate it would have been built with solid walls but all wall surfaces in this house between sash windows and pilasters, on both floors, are fitted with operable jalousies to provide the ultimate in ventilation.

From the high gabled window in the roof, the owner of this house could observe the arrival of his ships in Kingston Harbour.

MICO Institution was originally established on Hanover Street but, in 1894, the Trustees bought Quebec Lodge, north or Racecourse, changing the name to MICO Training College. Since then, it has become one of the principal teachers training colleges in the West Indies.

The 1907 earthquake destroyed the original building and, in 1910, a fire did severe damage. The present building was erected in 1911, the ground floor being much as it was before. Laid out in an 'L' shape with the clock tower at the apex, all the newer buildings have been tastefully erected behind this one.

Cleared of its Victorian gothic tower and other Victorian detail, the present 1911 building, has a good clean functional design, well suited to the tropics and the needs of the people of the region which it serves.

It is good to note that in spite of expense, current roof repairs are being carefully carried out with the traditional cedar shingles.

3 CHERRY GARDENS GREAT HOUSE, St. Andrew

This superb Georgian Great House with its fine proportions and beautiful detailing, has been a private home for centuries. Col Ezekiel Gomersal was acquiring adjoining parcels of land in the area from 1696 and the original house was built before 1714. It remained with different branches of the Dickenson family until 1845 when George William Gordon — who has become a Jamaican National Hero — bought it and settled it on his wife, to satisfy her dower rights. This was a fortunate move as it thereby escaped the liquidation of his assets when he was executed.

The next owner was Col Oscar Marescaux who paid £1,250 for the property. He was a man of great influence and an enthusiastic gardener. He extensively improved the house, collecting most of the antique furniture that is there today. He died in 1926 but in November 1929 the property was acquired by the Durie family and it has been their home since then. An insurance company now plans to develop it, on exclusive residential lines, but the Great House is scheduled for preservation under the Jamaica National Trust Law.

The interior of the house is most attractively furnished and contains some outstanding pieces of antique Jamaican furniture, including the Port Royal sideboard and other fine mahogany pieces. The famous crystal chandelier has three tiers of crystal pendants and twenty six cut-glass branches, each carrying a light.

Buildings in Jamaica in the old days were always sited to catch all the prevailing breezes and here the louvred walls and louvred shutters, behind the windows. make the most of this natural ventilation. All the external doors are sanded — for maximum weather protection and to discourage termites.

Anghelen - 79

4 VALE ROYAL, Montrose Road, St. Andrew

This house has become the official residence of the Prime Minister of Jamaica and is one of the oldest continuously occupied homes in the island.

Said to have been built about 1694, known then as Prospect Pan, it has undergone much reconditioning without its character being destroyed. The driveway until about 1926, ran for all but a mile in a straight line to Trafalgar Road, flanked on both sides with Royal Palms, hence Vale Royal.

The Hon. Simon Taylor, the first recorded owner, was said to have been the wealthiest landed proprietor in Jamaica in his day. He was Custos of St.Thomas-in-the-East, long time member of the House of Assembly, General of the Militia and he entertained lavishly at Vale Royal. Among his more illustrious guests were Admiral Lord Nelson and General and Lady Nugent. He died in 1813.

There were a number of later owners but in 1928 government bought the house as the official residence of the Colonial Secretary — though it also continued as the home of at least one former mistress who's duppy (or ghost) still haunts it!

This old house has a number of architectural features. The lookout on the top gives a view of Port Royal but it also acts as a vent through the centre of the building. The deep verandahs and extended roof over the windows are also for coolness. The ornate diamond shaped panes in the windows are most unusual in Jamaica.

The wing, extending to the left of the main house, is a modern addition containing a banqueting hall. The tasteful manner in which it is designed is a perfect example of how modern architecture can be made compatible with the old. Sadly, this is not often attained.

5 OAKTON, Half Way Tree, St.Andrew

This fine residence was probably built around the middle of the last century. Soldiers marching from Spanish Town, the capital, to their camp in the Blue Mountains, to escape malaria on the plains, would halt for a rest in the shade of the 'half-way-tree' a few chains from here.

No record has been found to indicate the original owner but at one time it was an exclusive school run by Miss Bovell and Mrs. Van Koolenburg ran it as a guest house in the 1920s. It then became the home of W.E. Powell whose famous bakery was a few chains up the road near the present clock tower. In the 1930s his heirs sold it to Kingston and St. Andrew Council and it was used as a fire station until the 1960s.

This wooden house, with its gracefully curving dual stairway, supported by red brick arches, is particularly well designed. Another of similar design on East Race Course in Kingston is better known but lacks the delicate lines seen here. The fretted transomes, inside and outside, over the doors, are of unusual geometric pattern and are very clean cut.

The balance of this building is very pleasing but it is also thoroughly functional with its louvred walls and its side verandahs with wide overhangs to keep off sun and rain. The red brick undercraft was originally open, with arches on all sides, to create natural ventilation beneath the wooden floor of the living quarters above. When converted to offices, the ground had to be excavated to create adequate headroom and steps lead down to the lower floor level inside.

The KSAC Traffic Department is now based here and it is gratifying to find that many of the staff appreciate this worthy example of Jamaica's architectural heritage and, significantly, to see that the original brass knocker on the front door is still in use. The entry from the road is central to the front of the house and was originally graced by some magnificent iron gates.

BRANCH OF
TRAFFIC ENG.D

AngheLen - '82

6 TRAFALGAR HOUSE, St. Andrew

The original property house was built about 1810 and belonged to a series of prominent legal men. It was sold to Government as the residence for the Army Commander, when the capital of Jamaica was moved from Spanish Town to Kingston in 1895. At Independence in 1962, the British Government acquired it as the official residence of the British High Commissioner.

In 1907, the earthquake destroyed the house but it was rebuilt on somewhat different lines, incorporating some of the design details. However the older house had all its living accommodation on the upper level, access being by external double stairway at each side of a central portico, sited where the upstairs verandah now stands. The lower level then consisted of an arched undercroft containing mainly storerooms and service rooms. The old kitchen was in an outhouse connected by an open-sided covered way, as was customary, but it was still in use in the 1960's.

The 1910 remodelling incorporated the ground floor as part of dwelling, in keeping with the times, with open verandahs giving access to the garden. Inside the front doors, a mahogany staircase now leads to the bedrooms graced by a large painting of HM the Queen.

The extensive use of wooden jalousies not only offers excellent ventilation, but also helps to give the building a lower profile so that it blends better with the gardens surrounding it. The use of a pediment over the triple bank of louvres, on each side of the entrance, are an unusual touch, but there may have been sash windows there at an earlier stage.

7 EBONY GLADES, St. Andrew

This pretty house, with its red brick courtyard, is not an old one. It has belonged to several well known Jamaican families including Elders and Melhados, before its present owners.

A number of well proved architectural elements have been incorporated in its construction. The shingled walls provide insulation and weather protection but the chimneys are only decorative. The steel window bars, in lattice pattern, have louvred shutters outside but sidehung glass windows on the inside, to supply variable ventilation.

This house is a very practicable one for our Jamaican climate.

Anghelen - 82

8 DEMONTEVIN LODGE, Port Antonio

Early in this century this fine brick house was built by the Hon. David Sampson Gideon PC, CMG, MLC who became Custos of Portland in 1923. Born in New York in 1862, the same year his father died, he attended Kingston Collegiate College until, aged 14, he left to go into business. He was a prominent businessman in Port Antonio and later helped found the United Fruit Co. A man of great energy, he ardently promoted the cause of self government for Jamaica as early as 1902 in both the legislative and in London. He was consul for Spain from which his ancestors had fled the inquisition.

The name of his house probably had a family connection as he gave the name De Montevin to one of his sons. He was closely related to the Abandana family of Buff Bay. The present owner of the Lodge is J.A. Mullins who bought it in 1959. He and his wife run it as a guest house with an old-time Jamaican atmosphere.

This decorative Victorian building is very typical of the period but very unusual in Jamaica. It has few features that cater to this climate and they appear to be afterthoughts like the hoods on the windows and the swing louvre doors on the verandah.

The barley sugar columns, verandah rails and other ironwork, would probably have been shipped on banana boats collecting fruit. The arched carriage entrance, incorporated into the fabric of the house, is unusual but has its counterpart in an old building in Spanish Town where it is right on the street and hung with heavy wooden doors.

9 BUTCHER'S SHOP, Port Antonio

This functional building, with its covered walkway on the street and deep verandah above, is well shaded from the hot sun. The lattice along the front has the same effect in addition to being decorative.

Though not old, this house had reached a state of bad repair so that, a few years ago, Earl Levy remodelled it to show the towns-people how attractive it could look. The tracery of the verandah rails and fretwork ornamenting the gables are typical details and he had a plan to remodel the whole town on these lines. Unfortunately it has been delayed but his steady leadership in the field of archi-tectual design, especially in this part of the island, has been out-standing and his devoted efforts are an inspiration to others.

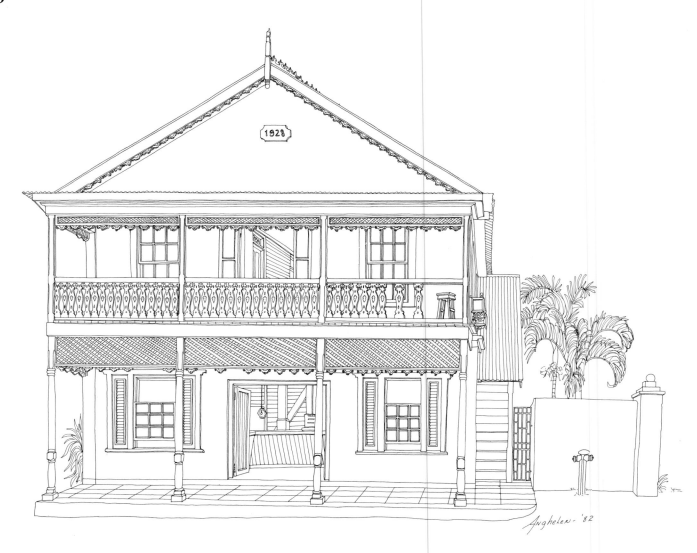

Anghelen - '82

10 THE RAILWAY STATION, Port Antonio

Port Antonio is at the end of the Jamaican Railway line in eastern Jamaica and this building, constructed in 1896, is typical of Jamaican railway architecture.

The waiting rooms, one for each class of travel, may be seen in the drawing and both windows and doors are fitted with small pieces of bright coloured glass casting colourful shadows within. At the other side of the building lie the train tracks and matching doors lead onto the platform alongside. The living quarters on the upper level would have housed the stationmaster and his family. When the banana trade was at its height, and Port Antonio a flourishing port, this station would have been a busy place.

11 THE COURT HOUSE, Port Antonio

This impressive brick building with its cutstone quoins was built in 1895 with some classic Georgian detail. The delicate design of its ironwork and its attractive perforated transomes, on the upper level, as well as the fine lines of the columns, create a most pleasing effect.

The rear of the building is almost identical in design to the front, facing the sea, but it is seldom seen as this frontage faces straight down the main street in Port Antonio's principal shopping area.

Anghelen - '82

12 NASEBERRY INN, Galina, Port Maria, St. Mary

Sir Noel Coward lived not far from here at 'Firefly', where he is buried, and he opened an arts and craft shop in this house which could be mistaken for many similar ones around the island but, in fact, no two are exactly the same. It is difficult to imagine a house like this without its decorative embelishments and it is the gingerbread designs, in all their many variations, which have the greatest effect.

The hexagonal corner of the verandah with its pointed roof adds distinction, as does the bay window on the front and louvred cooler extending at the left of the building. The original roofing material would have been cedar shingles instead of the unfortunate corrugated metal. This natural cedar, which can be seen on the left roof peak, helps the building blend with its surrounding vegetation.

13 RACECOURSE, Oracabessa

This house belongs to Cecily Norton and was probably built around 1930. Houses of this style and layout are to be found in many parts of Jamaica. In fact, they borrow from many different styles, to provide good practical homes that stand up well to the climate of the island.

The bay window catches the breeze while the wide verandah gives good shade from the sun, cools the air passing across it, and keeps off the rain. Instead of windows, the numerous doors with their half rounded upper glass panels, open flat against the wall to give maximum ventilation from floor to ceiling. When closed at night, their latticed transoms keep the air circulating inside the house.

14 STORE, Oracabessa

The Carty family built two identical buildings to this, side by side, separated by a carriageway which had an arch across it. The remains of this arch may be seen on the left of this drawing. Both were bought by Cecil Silvera for his two daughters but one had to be pulled away, as a later owner refused to repair it and it became derelict.

Miss Thelma Robinson, in business in Oracabessa since 1920, runs her dry goods store here but it was originally in the other building.

This country store, with living quarters above, has verandahs front and back. The front one protects the wooden staircase but, at the rear, the stone steps are open to the elements. This all-wood functional building, with its 'herringbone' doors and shutters is nicely decorated with 'ginger-bread' trimmings.

A two foot extension beyond the verandah, on the right of the building, has its own roof and now houses a tailor's shop. It may have originally been built as a washroom with jug and basin but the privy would have been down the back yard.

15 NEUVILLE, Oracabessa

This "upstairs house", with its well balanced design, was built about 1922 by Isacher Sigismond Magnus JP, wharfowner. His six children were all born here.

Houses in this style may be seen in many parts of Jamaica, their spacious verandahs shielding them from sun and rain. The fretted design of the verandah rail is traditional as is that used in the door transoms, to give ventilation. The gable window looks out to sea.

Since this drawing was completed, a new owner has unfortunately filled in the ground floor verandah, between the columns, with concrete blocks, thus destroying the character of this old family house.

Anghelen - 82

16 RIO NUEVO GREAT HOUSE, St. Mary

Near this house was fought the decisive battle for Jamaica between the Spaniards and the English and it is likely that a much older building once stood on this site.

Here we see the typical layout of the Jamaican house which shows signs of a built-in verandah at each side — to accommodate bathrooms. The outside double sided staircase and external kitchen, with brick oven and chimney, in separate detached building, joined to the main house by a covered way, are typical features.

The fanlights and louvred doors provide maximum ventilation — that vital factor for comfortable living in a tropical climate.

AngheLen - 82

17 HARMONY HALL, St.Mary

This was the original property house on a small pimento estate in the latter part of the 19th century. Limes and pimento were the main crops and one can still see the old barbeques where allspice was dried in the sun.

At the turn of the century, this house became the manse for the local Methodist Circuit and the distinguished Sherlock family was one that lived there. To the right of the wide wooden swing gate to the entrance, stood a large freestanding letter box with door and lock. Rev. Parnther, who lived here in the early thirties, would have long remembered the visit of his twin Helwig nephews, age 9, for one locked the other in the letter box!

This property later became the private home of the Lobban family, for nearly fifty years, until they sold it in 1980 to the present owners.

On the floor is the "Kings Arms", pub and restaurant. Up the stone staircase is a spacious Gallery handling works of local artists and boutiques that sell the best in Jamaican handicrafts.

The restoration of this building illustrates perfectly how good design, good taste, and good workmanship can enhance an existing structure. Under the guidance of architect Ben Eales of CAST, this building was repaired, restored, and vastly improved, retaining its strong basic lines and exposing the stone surfaces. The intricate fretwork of the gingerbread trimmings and balustrade were designed by Dawn Scott, the noted batik artist, and specially produced on the property by local craftsmen.

The group of dedicated people behind this project hope others will follow in their footsteps.

18 BONE COTTAGE, 86 Main Street, Ocho Rios

Home of Lena Scott for over twenty years, this simple house, with its nicely balanced frontage, is raised for coolness well above the ground level — a traditional feature.

Similarly, the fenestration follows the West Indian tradition of double hung sash with a narrow serpentine jalousie at each side. The former provides up to fifty per cent clear opening and the latter, one hundred percent, to keep the inside of the house cool. Whereas the glass in the sashes will create heat within, when the sun strikes it, the louvres actually deflect the sun's rays making them the ideal window treatment for this sunny climate.

19 ROSEDALE, (Little Great House), Ocho Rios

By 1958 "Rosedale" was scheduled for demolition by the Parish Council because it was derelict.

In 1959 Dr. Bob Page bought the property and, by 1960, it had been completely restored by a dedicated group of local craftsmen he had assembled — mainly from the former Temple Galleries in Montego Bay.

The Galleries Workshop was created at Ocho Rios and a showroom for their products, consisting of furniture and furniture miniatures, was established in the upper floor of this house which was renamed "The Little Great House". Below was an attractive restaurant and bar which still functions there as the Little Pub.

This modest house was carefully restored. The hoods across the tops of the windows were there before but were not shingled ones. The vertically hung shingles, which cover the walls of the upper storey, were fully replaced. This interesting architectural feature, though not widely used, may be seen in other parts of the island and probably stems from Europe. Here they provide excellent weather protection and good insulation from the tropical heat.

Anghelen - 82

Wrapped around its own hill, like a spiral, is the driveway to this spacious house. Its solid stone foundations show signs of a fortified room with gun slots from 18th Century. Its early history is vague but, in 1910, Sir John Pringle, PC, MLC, bought it for his daughter Minna Simpson JP but she did not move in until 1925.

Like her father, she had a vibrant personality, was a pioneer of the co-operative movement and considered a bit of a revolutionary in her day. At 8:30 am each day, prayers were held for house and field staff and afterwards problems on the property discussed. From this, the Lucky Hill Co-operative Farm evolved and today flourishes. In the old outbuildings you see new machines. An operator happens to be secretary of the Community Centre and Captain of the Cricket team. On a hill across the valley stands the Community Centre and a new musical group is practising there.

This old house has seen dramatic changes in its time. At the centre is the large dining hall with bedrooms opening out from it. The extensive verandahs and pepperpot roofs were added by Sir John but the basic house behind these is a traditional Jamaican one constructed with Spanish wall. The double sided entrance steps are built from local cutstone.

21 MOUNT PLENTY, St. Ann

John Hiatt, Custos of St. Ann owned this property early in the last century and his family burial ground is nearby. Since then, it has belonged to the Cameron and Roxborough families, then Lord Brownlow and Bernard Cooke, and now ot it is the home of Dorothy and Howard Shirley.

One day, during Elsie Roxborough's regime, a strange foreign couple came to call on her to discuss spanish treasure. Certainly the early spanish settlers knew St.Ann well and many caches of pieces-of-eight have been found over the years. She did not consider the discussion of any importance until one of her cattle men came next morning to say that, during the night, a large rectangular hole had been dug down on the common.

The fabric of the house is spanish walling above the cutstone lower level which shows signs of a fortified room. Before the verandahs were built in, this was a house with few rooms. A later expansion incorporated a master bedroom and gable windows were added. Inside is some fine woodwork including some beautiful doors.

The double stairway, in the foreground of this drawing, leads across the portico directly into what is now the dining room, which is not unusual in Jamaica. The rest of the house seen here, was exposed verandah with turned bullet tree columns supporting the roof. These are still intact, between the windows and jalousies, and behind the vertically hung sanded shingles below, which are cut to an unusual wedge shape on the lower edges.

Anghelen - '80

During the last century John Wilson Davis owned this and many other local properties but, at Belmont, he kept his mistress Sarah Davis Scott. She died here in 1855 age 60 and is buried under a fine marble tombstone nearby which extols her virtues and has his name boldly engraved upon it. It is not known who built the house but it is eighteenth century and there have been a number of other owners.

The overseer for many of these owners was Hubert Goldsmith who lived in this house nearly seventy years. His responsibilities included the supervision of Dunns River Falls which are part of this property, until government took over in the late 1960s.

The approach to the house is through a gateway in a stone wall. The broad entrance steps, supported by well designed triple arches, were once topped by a portico to protect the front door. Inside is the front parlour and, although the house is now in a very dilapidated state, the mahogany wall panelling with wallpaper above can still be seen.

Across the barbeque to the left of this drawing is a group of stone outbuildings including a kitchen, storerooms, a three seater privy, and a lockup from slavery days, with heavy chains let into the wall.

It is hoped that UDC, the present owners, will undertake restoration of this house, before it is too late.

23 WINDSOR ROAD, St. Ann's Bay

This attractive country house, on the outskirts of St. Ann's Bay, may have been built as the lodge for Windsor Great House, up on the hill. Locally, it has long been known just as "The Lodge" and, in the 1920s, this house and the Great House were, in fact, both owned by a Mr. Cameron.

Mr. Kenneth Perkins lived here for over forty years and his daughters still do so. When his brother died, his teenage nephew, Wilmot Perkins, the well known journalist, moved in too and he was brought up here as one of the family.

The living quarters are located on the upper level in the traditional manner, mainly to catch the prevailing breezes. Although this appears to be a wooden house this is not so as the lower level is built with thick cutstone walls and, from floor to roof level, at each side, are red bricks. At the rear may be seen the red brick kitchen with brick chimney, away from the house, where all the cooking was done in the old days.

Below the verandah level, the area which is now enclosed was probably store rooms and other offices. The fretted baluster and trims known as gingerbread give a light decorative touch to this late nineteenth century country house. There may have been an older building standing on these same foundations.

The Cardiff Hall property was ceded to Daniel Blagrove by Cromwell as a reward for his part in the regicide of King Charles 1st. He was the only man never made to pay for his crime.

Although this is only the busha's house, it is built entirely of cutstone. The famous great house up on the hill, its chapel and slave hospital, and its unusual stone gate-houses, with pepperpot roofs, are all of similar style, fine design, and of high quality masonry work. If, as seems likely, the same master builder was responsible for all these buildings then a plaque set into the wall of the great house and engraved 'Forsyte' may well identify him.

In this house the original wide floor boards ceiling boards, and door jambs are still in place. The walled-in window opening in front never carried a window, possibly to avoid window tax.

In front of the house can be seen an old copper boiler such as was used in the distillery at the sugar works, to distill the sugar from cane juice.

25 FLORENCE HALL, Trelawny

This small house, built with cutstone throughout, as are its kitchen and other outhouses at the rear, lies within a mile of Rock — the original waterfront area for Martha Brae when it was the parish capital — and Florence Hall sugar property had its own wharf there.

Though there may have been a larger great house on the property — only the steps remain — an advertisement in the Royal Gazette in May 1780 describes it as a sugar property then.

In 1859, on the owner's death, a dispute arose within the family as to its ownership. Unfortunately the factions came to blows and, with their followers, the Florence Hall Riots took place. They were eventually subdued by the militia.

The fine quality of the masonry as well as the simple basic design distinguish this building. The heavy stonework does not give a feeling of heaviness due partially to the proportions of the building but also to the delicate gingerbread trimmings and the intricate design of the verandah rails. The gentle sweep of the roof and the fine lines of the verandah columns also contribute to the charm of this attractive house.

Anghelen '82

In 1779, this house was built by Edward Barrett of Cinnamon Hill, who, like the other wealthy planters of his day, built a splendid town house in Falmouth, the new capital of the newly created Parish of Trelawny. The town, laid out on a Georgian grid plan, on his lands, had this prime site at the bottom of Market Street and even today one can see signs of the former grandeur of this house.

The lower part is cutstone, the upstairs of wood overhanging it, supported by six timber columns, creating a deep shaded piazza which, until recent years, was paved with flagstones. The draught of air, passing through the piazza, helped to cool the reception rooms above. The external stairway gave callers direct access to the upstairs salon, without passing through the rest of the house.

The principal drawing room has some unusually decorative doorways, in the Adam style, hung with heavy mahogany panel doors. There are dados around the important rooms and cedar panelling and folded louvre shutters are hung on the inside of the graceful triple hung sash windows which run down to the floor.

Two of the five wrought iron balconies of the Regency design, needed replacing so they were removed and sent to Kingston to be copied. But that was in 1951 and unfortunately reached there on the eve of the terrible hurricane. They were never seen again and since then, only two remain in place. They were imported from Philadelphia originally.

This house became a Methodist Manse for many years and still belongs to the church. Sadly, lack of funds has prevented proper repairs to be effected. The situation is now desperate and Jamaica is about to lose yet another important part of its Architectural Heritage unless action is taken now.

Anghelen – '82

27 THE POST OFFICE, Market Street, Falmouth

This well designed building with its pleasing proportions and cleancut details has recently been re-roofed with traditional cedar shakes. Note the cap and comb — a typical Jamaican feature — on the top of the roof. There are matching arches at each end of the shady piazza with deep quoins similar to those on the corners of the building.

The louvred shutters were recently fitted by the film company producing "Eureka". Authentic townscape of the 18th/19th century is not easy to find and Market Street, Falmouth, still appears much as it did in the last century, whereas most towns have only individual buildings left. It constitutes, therefore, an important part of Jamaica's architectual heritage that should be scrupuously maintained and protected.

28 21 DUKE STREET, Falmouth

This solid brick house stands at the corner of Duke and Queen Streets, on the main northcoast road through the town. This building is one of the best of its kind in the island, illustrative of the early Georgian style but suggestive of the Queen Anne period.

Its yellow bricks would have come here as ballast on a sailing ship calling for sugar at the then busy port of Falmouth.

The latticed porch adds a light touch to this rather stolid building. The looped iron railing which originally stood on the front wall on Duke Street — instead of the pierced blocks — and also the original cedar roof, with its predominantly horizontal lines, would have had a similar effect.

This building, now used as government offices, belongs to the Whiting family.

29 GREENWOOD GREAT HOUSE, St. James

The Hon. Richard Barrett (1789 - 1839) Speaker of the House of Assembly, Custos of St. James, and one of the leading landed proprietors, had this house built for him by Philip Morris, his father-in-law, in the early 1800s, primarily for entertaining. He was cousin to the Barretts of Cinnamon Hill and Falmouth and also to the famous poetess, Elizabeth Barrett-Browning of Wimpole Street in London.

Man of many parts, he once won a £100 prize for the best constructed mile of the, then new, macadamised road in the island. It was at Greenwood between Montego Bay and Falmouth.

The present owners, Bob and Ann Betton, have a fine collection of antique furniture including some Barrett heirlooms and some fascinating music making machines, like a barrel organ, which they play to visitors.

High above the coast road stands this cutstone Great House with sweeping views along the coast to the horizon, the curve of the earth being clearly visible from this vantage point.

The jalousie walls on the ground floor, the window hoods, gable vent, and the louvred cooler above, all help to cool the house as do the wide verandahs which also help protect the house from the impact of northers. The wide flagstones used on floors and steps and bricks used to build the arch let into the house to support the verandah stairs, would have come to Jamaica from England, as ballast on sailing ships, collecting hogsheads of sugar.

Anghelen '82

30 ROSEHALL GREAT HOUSE, St. James

This beautiful house was built about 1750 by George Ash for John Palmer, Custos of St. James, for £30,000, a huge sum in those days.

The legend tells of an infamous mistress of Rosehall who dabbled in witch-craft, held orgies, and went through a series of husbands and lovers who died mys-teriously. Her name was Annie, not to be mistaken for Rosa who died in 1790 and whose good works are commemorated on a decorative plaque in the Parish church.

The fine proportions of this cut stone house are typical of the Georgian period but few of Jamaica's Great Houses were as well executed as this. Matching pavilions once stood at each side of the main building.

The imposing frontage has broad stone steps starting in one flight and rising in two to the terraced entrance. Each flight is supported by beautiful cut stone arches in the traditional manner

The stone work to be seen in the walls, quoins, windows, doorways and arches, are of very fine workmanship. Though a ruin for many years, in 1966 Rosehall was bought by John Rollins, the present owner, and plans to rebuild were put in hand.

He commissioned the late Mr. Tom Concannon, whose ability and experience as a conservation architect were rare, and his faithful restoration work on this project is outstanding.

The interiors including the mahogany staircase, which he completely rebuilt, are a tribute to Jamaican craftsmen of the past and a great credit to those of today. Visitors are admitted.

31 ROUND HOUSE, Montego Bay

This charming brick house is just above the main square in Montego Bay and stands at the corner of Union Street and Orange Street on a private property known as 'Georgian Square'. At the diagonally opposite corner in the main house, of two stories in cutstone, with an outside stone staircase. A one time owner built this brick gem for his mistress.

Since then it has changed hands several times and, until recently, was the Montego Bay showroom of Douglas Cooper, the international jeweller. He made many improvements to the property and greatly enhanced its appearance, and the owner, Muff Charley, is determined to protect its character.

It is now occupied by Ky-Ann Walker who runs an attractive Gallery in the house for the sale of paintings, and objets d'arts.

Anghelen -'82

32 CRYSTAL COTTAGE, Duke Street, Montego Bay

One of the first owners of this house was Bob Watt and it may have been specially built for him. He and then, later, his nephew, Emerson Watt Parkin — who married the girl next door — lived here for a period extending over fifty years. The present owner is Samuel Spence.

This attractive wooden cottage, painted white with bright blue trimmings, incorporates some particularly intricate gingerbread details suggestive of furniture design. Not surprisingly, the builder Mr. Jennings, who built several wooden houses in this, then new, residential area of the town, was also a cabinet maker.

In fact, over sixty years ago, a young lady — coincidentally, living just across the road at 'Adara' — was given a beautiful marquetry box made by the same Mr. Jennings and she still cherishes it today: it was an engagement present from her future husband.

It is common practise in this climate to have open transomes over doors, but in this house, they are repeated over the windows too and extend in a broad band all round the building, just below the eaves of the roof. Their complex tracery pattern is also worthy of note as is the rare use of turned finials on the upper edge of the verandah, an area more commonly fitted with lattice work. The ornamental design of the gingerbread under the gable, once again, shows great originality.

33 GROVE HILL HOUSE, Montego Bay

Grove Hill House built in the eighteenth century is one of the oldest in Montego Bay. Like several other local families, the Brown family who owns it, came here to escape Cromwell as they were Royalists. George Samuel Phillpotts Brown was born here in 1838 and died in 1896. Unfortunately, earlier births have not been recorded, but Lt. Horatio Nelson was a guest here in 1795. From the iron balcony off the withdrawing room, just to the left of this view, which overlooks the harbour, he signalled to one of his ships that had caught fire. Other famous visitors were Josiah Spode and more recently, amongst others, Winston Churchill, Lord Beaverbrook and Somerset Maugham.

Where the new wing now stands, but built into the ground, was the hurricane shelter. In it were three months supply of cured food with wine and water in Spanish jars and yabbas. When the town below, flooded, the town's people knew they could look for shelter and food at Grove Hill. Like Orange Street, its name comes from its orange groves, but there was a thick vine of grapes over the steps; cows, chickens and bees were kept on this property.

Unlike many of the old Great Houses, this one is still kept up as a home by the family and its present owner is "Muff" Charley nee Phillpotts Brown.

The cut stone for the lower floor and the flagstones on the terrace came as ballast on sailing ships from Cornwall and the iron railings also came from England. The columns are the original ones made from blind-eye hardwood and, like the cedar shingles on the upper floors, they are painted and sanded every year. The louvres and coolers are green, like the railings and the pyramid topped brick columns around the yard and among the many old out houses are white washed and give the property a very neat appearance.

Anghelen - 82

34 COTTON TREE HOUSE, Union Street, Montego Bay

In 1834 Grezell Phillips, the owner, had this property surveyed. The plan shows only the original house centred on the front door. Directly below, down many steps, under the huge cotton tree was the Union Street entrance, where legend sites a slave market. The plan dispels this as it shows a large carriage house on one side of the gates and balancing it on the other side are stables.

For most of this century three generations of the Rerrie family have occupied the house but they have not been alone . . . it seems that a lady wearing a hat decorated with cherries has appeared at times and also there have sometimes been sounds of clanging chains!

The built-in verandah on the right of the drawing was open to the garden until about thirty years ago and the porch on the left, at one time the East Street entrance, is now a bathroom.

The construction of the lower level is stone but columns of brick support the upstairs which is the living area. This is constructed of Spanish walling with mortar outside and lined with tongue and grooved boards within, giving excellent insulation. The roof overhang is very narrow for Jamaica but Captain Rerrie recalls there were louvred coolers outside the windows, protecting the windows and which, for washing hands, held jug and basin for water that was emptied through the slatted cooler.

The gable windows are in a loft but between it and some rooms below, are lattices in the ceiling which provide light and ventilation.

35 THE TOWN HOUSE, Montego Bay

This fine Georgian Townhouse built of red brick, is one of the best in Jamaica. Built around the end of the eighteenth century as a private residence, it was later put to other use. At one period it was a hotel and, at another, the upper floor became the first synagogue in Montego Bay. Then, for over fifty years, it was a Masonic Lodge.

In 1967, Nigel Pemberton bought the building from a group of people headed by Lady Sarah Churchill. He completely restored it, removing the long wooden verandah which ran the whole length of the building. The red bricks, protected by stucco, were exposed and repointed and the lower level, under the house, was fully excavated and built-in to accommodate the existing restaurant. This is entered from the rear of the building, across old flagstones and down a few steps. The restaurant proprietors are Jim and Julia Snead.

Anghelen- '82

36 42 MARKET STREET, Montego Bay

This wooden house was built in an almost classic Jamaican design. Similar houses to this one, built about 1910, may be seen with the same basic layout in many parts of the island.

The variable factor in this style of house lies in the quality and design of the gingerbread and its frequent combination with lattices to give a distinctive character to the building. This house belongs to Vernal Campbell and is occupied by designer Trevor Owen.

Anghelen '82

37 ROEHAMPTON GREAT HOUSE, St. James

Built in the mid 1700s this fine building has a commanding view on all sides. In 1831, it was the residence of John Baillie, when it was his sugar property. By 1914 Philip Ogilvie had bought it but he died shortly afterwards from a horse-riding accident.

It now belongs to the 4-H Club Movement as a centre for its activities in the area.

This house is large and square and it is built to monumental scale. Inside there are some pleasing mahogany details including a wide staircase. There are four entrance porches, one on each side. The construction is from cutstone and the cedar shingle roof is built in two parts with a gutter to reduce the height and thereby wind resistant

This building is listed by Jamaica National Trust which has, in the past, done repairs to it.

38 THE COURT HOUSE, Lucea, Hanover

This fine Court House was probably built early in the 19th century. The lower floor is constructed with cut stone, incorporating an arcaded piazza over the sidewalk. Extending over it, built with wood siding, and sanded, is the upper level that houses the actual courtroom and offices. There is a stone staircase inside.

The cupola is fitted with a clock which was not originally intended for this building or even for this town. In fact it was shipped here in error instead of to the island of St. Lucia, a thousand miles away. The same clock maker, in England, had orders for both places and this much larger time piece — the face is nearly five feet high — came to Jamaica. It was left in Lucea for so many years that it was eventually decided to make use of it so the cupola was redesigned to accommodate it.

39 SHOP, Main Street, Lucea, Hanover

This old wooden house
dates back to the latter half of the
nineteenth century, built by a
Mr. Gardner, it was later bought
by Alan Hogg, then the Dickson
family, and now Gladys Johnson
owns it. It was designed for a
merchant so he could carry on
his business downstairs and live
upstairs.

Note the four fluted columns
upstairs, which, with latticework,
fretted transomes, and gingerbread
at the eaves of the roof, all add·to
the charm of this old building.
The wooden panelling at each side
of the verandah really looks as if
it should be on the inside of the
house but, used in this way it can
be appreciated by others.

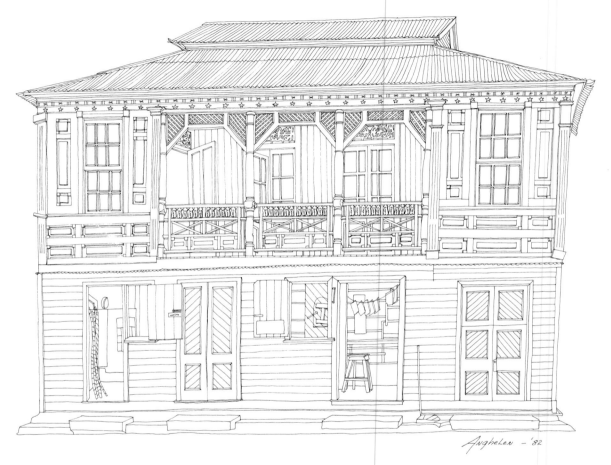

40 MANNING'S SCHOOL, Savanna-la-Mar, Westmoreland

Thomas Manning in 1710 created an endowment for the establishment of a free school in the parish of Westmoreland. The endowment consisted of a property, cattle, slaves and produce off the property but the school did not open until 1738.

This building, though not the original school, was built as the school house and is still in full use as part of a greatly expanded institution. This distinctive building, with its deep gable roof and belfry and its generous porches and verandahs, is built in the style of the late nineteenth century.

ACKNOWLEDGEMENTS

I wish to thank the following people who helped to make my stay both enjoyable and possible:

Oliver Clarke, Tony Clarke, Lady Sarah Churchill, Mayor Kenneth Diacre, Graham Davis, Frank Dixon, Josef Forstmayr, Colin Garland, Richard Issa, Earl Levy, Audrey McHardy, Sandy Morris, Hon. Val Parnell, Annabella Ogden, Martin Orr, Patricia and Geoffrey Pinto, Peter Proudlock, Lloyd Reckord, Dawn Scott, Morley Speed and Peter Stephenson.

Also all who helped in the production of this book.

Anghelen Arrington Phillips

All the owners and occupiers of these houses have been most helpful in supplying information and I am most indebted to them.

I would also like to thank all the other people who have helped me including:

John Aarons, Dorrit Browne, Basil Burke, Bernard Cooke, Pat Cooke, Emma Curtin, Marguerite Curtin, Graham Davis, Dolly Dayes, Fiona Edwards, Oswald Goldsmith, David Gray, Richard Issa, Earl Levy, Prudence Lovell, Angus MacDonald, Audrey de S. Pinto, Deborah de S. Pinto, Patricia Pinto, Luna Walter, Burnett Webster.

Acknowledgement is also due to:

The National Library of Jamaica
The Georgian Society of Jamaica
The Jamaica Historical Society
"Dictionary of Place Names"
    by Inez Sibley
"Exploring Jamaica" by Wright
    and White

Geoffrey de Sola Pinto